Information Systems E   ...ry

Migrating from SSADM Version 3 to Version 4

Janet Blowers O'Neill

CCTA
April 1992
LONDON: HMSO

© Crown Copyright 1992

Applications for reproduction should be made to HMSO

First published 1992

ISBN 0 11 330576 1

For further information regarding this publication and other CCTA products please contact:

Library
Riverwalk House
157-161 Millbank
London SW7P 4RT

071-217 3331

Contents

Foreword

1	**Introduction**	**1**
	1.1 Purpose of this volume	
	1.2 Who should read this volume	
	1.3 The structure of this volume	
	1.4 How to use this volume	
2	**Overview**	**3**
	2.1 SSADM	
	2.2 Why migrate to SSADM Version 4?	
	2.3 Improvements to SSADM Version 4	
	2.4 The impact of migration	
	2.5 Planning for migration	
3	**Technical overview of SSADM Version 4**	**5**
	3.1 Design objectives of SSADM Version 4	
	3.2 Key features of SSADM Version 4	
	3.3 New and changed techniques	
	3.4 Changes to the method	
	3.5 SSADM Version 4 documentation	
4	**Issues to be considered before migration**	**15**
	4.1 Effective delivery of systems	
	4.2 Benefits, costs and opportunities	
	4.3 Effective planning for migration	
	4.4 Project management considerations	
	4.5 SSADM Version 4 training	
	4.6 SSADM Version 4 skills	

4.7 Project support

4.8 Standards

4.9 SSADM Version 3 maintenance

5 **Developing a migration plan for the organisation 27**

5.1 Where you are now

5.2 Where do you want to be?

5.3 How to get there

6 **Migration of SSADM projects** 29

6.1 Approaches to migrating the organisation's projects to SSADM Version 4

6.2 Project by project basis

6.3 All new projects move to SSADM Version 4

6.4 All projects migrate to Version 4 at once (big bang approach)

6.5 Choosing projects for migration

6.6 Adopting Version 4 on individual projects

6.7 Adopting new Version 4 techniques within a Version 3 structure

6.8 Using elements of the Version 4 structure with Version 3 techniques

6.9 Adopting Version 4 during a project's life (cut-over points)

7 **Checklist** 43

Annexes 45

A Re-documentation necessary for each suggested cut-over point

Bibliography 59

Glossary 61

Foreword

The **Information Systems Engineering Library** provides guidance on carrying out Information Systems Engineering activities. In the IS lifecycle, Information Systems Engineering takes place once the IS Strategy has been defined. It is concerned with the development of information systems up to the operational stage, when an information system becomes the responsibility of infrastructure management.

The Information Systems Engineering Library builds on the guidance in the CCTA IS Guides B set: *Developing Information Systems* and complements other CCTA products, in particular the IS project management method, PRINCE, and the systems analysis and design method, SSADM.

The Information Systems Engineering Library will be of interest to IS providers, helping them to improve the quality and productivity of their IS development work. It will also be of interest to business managers, whose business operations depend on having effective IS support by means of Information Systems Engineering activities.

CCTA welcomes customer views on Information Systems Engineering Library publications. Please send your comments to:

> Customer Services
> Information Systems Engineering Group
> Gildengate House
> Upper Green Lane
> Norwich NR3 1DW

Migrating from SSADM Version 3 to Version 4

Acknowledgements

The assistance of Cathy Morton under contract to CCTA from Model Systems Ltd is gratefully acknowledged.

Chapter 1
Introduction

1 Introduction

1.1 Purpose of this volume

Structured Systems Analysis and Design Method (SSADM) is the UK government's preferred method for the systems analysis and design of IT based information systems. SSADM Version 4 has been developed to meet the needs of systems development in the 90s.

This volume is intended to help to make an informed decision on migration from SSADM Version 3 to Version 4. It offers advice and guidance on the benefits to be realised and the issues to be resolved when considering migration to SSADM Version 4. The volume also provides details of the improvements from SSADM Version 3 to Version 4.

1.2 Who should read this volume

This volume is intended for people who are responsible for information systems development, policy and practice.

The guidance will be of particular interest to *managers responsible for making the migration decision*. They need to understand the issues associated with migration to Version 4. To understand these issues they need information about the benefits, costs and opportunities of migration and the impact of their decision. There will be implications for technical and human resource policies, for IS investment planning, for the management and control of IS operations, and of course for IS development projects themselves.

The volume will also be of interest to *project managers* of teams using SSADM and to *practitioners* currently using SSADM Version 3. For project managers it provides guidance on the migration of existing projects. It also helps them to identify the changes to the method that facilitate project management.

For SSADM practitioners this volume provides information on the impact of changes in the technical deliverables to be produced and the techniques to produce them.

1.3	**The structure of this volume**	Chapter 2 provides an overview of SSADM Version 4, the benefits to be realised and the impact of a migration decision. Chapter 3 describes the main features of SSADM Version 4. Management issues are set out in Chapter 4, followed by advice on developing a migration plan in Chapter 5. Technical considerations are described in Chapter 6, with a checklist in Chapter 7.
1.4	**How to use this volume**	This volume has been developed primarily for an audience that is familiar with SSADM Version 3. It is not designed as an introduction to SSADM Version 4 for readers who are new to SSADM. The volume gives broad guidance about how migration may be accomplished; readers should apply this guidance to suit their particular needs.

All readers should look at Chapter 2 for an overview of SSADM Version 4 and the major issues relating to a migration decision.

Managers responsible for making the migration decision will find the relevant management issues in Chapter 4. Managers who need to develop a migration plan should also read Chapters 5, 6 and 7.

Readers who are particularly interested in the technical details of improvements to SSADM Version 4 should read Chapter 3.

2 Overview

2.1 SSADM

SSADM is a method designed by CCTA as a systematic approach to the analysis and design of IT based information systems. It is the analysis and design method recommended for use in UK government departments. The method is non-proprietory, with a policy of open development and support.

2.2 Why migrate to SSADM Version 4?

Version 3 was designed to meet the systems analysis and design needs of the 80s, with the emphasis on batch processing. It is not ideally suited for designing on-line interactive systems and dealing with a range of implementation environments; it has limited capability for customisation. It has only limited support for the use of advanced tools such as application generators.

SSADM Version 4 is the current standard and maintained version of the method. It is the area of future investment by tools vendors and training organisations; it is becoming widely adopted in the open market and supported by many training and consultancy organisations and tools suppliers.

The development of Version 4 has been planned to intercept Euromethod and appropriate emerging standards.

2.3 Improvements to SSADM Version 4

SSADM Version 4 has resolved all these issues and provides a sound and reliable basis for exploiting future technical opportunities. It meets the needs of system development in the 90s in these ways:

- closer alignment with business need through user participation
- better support for project management with improved interfaces to project control
- improved specification for implementation of the designed system – complete, rigorous and formalised
- modular structure – making use, training and customisation of the method easier than before

- product driven approach with rigorous quality criteria to check that products have been produced correctly.

The technical details of improvements to SSADM Version 4 are described in Chapter 3.

2.4 The impact of migration

Before making a decision on migration, managers need to be able to assess the potential impact of their decision. They will need information on the likely costs and timescales if they decide to move to Version 4 – and they would also need to assess the implications if they decide to stay with Version 3. The issues vary depending on the cicumstances but include the following:

- ease and effectiveness of system analysis and design in the delivery of systems
- the benefits, costs and opportunities
- effective planning for migration
- project management considerations for Version 4 projects, such as project planning and project control
- Version 4 training and skills requirements
- availability of support, such as training, CASE tools and consultancy
- conformance to policies described in the organisation's IS strategy
- maintenance of Version 3 systems in a Version 4 environment.

These management issues are considered in Chapter 4.

2.5 Planning for migration

When planning to migrate to Version 4, it is important to be aware of the advantages to be gained from migrating existing projects at specific points in the SSADM lifecycle. Chapter 5 provides general guidance on the development of a migration plan. Chapter 6 provides specific guidance to help organisations to migrate projects at the right time for them.

For those who have decided to migrate to Version 4, Chapter 7 provides a checklist of the issues to be considered in putting together a migration plan.

3 Technical overview of SSADM Version 4

This chapter provides an overview of the main technical changes between SSADM Version 3 and Version 4.

3.1 Design objectives of SSADM Version 4

The following design objectives were set for SSADM Version 4:

- to maintain the existing strengths of SSADM
- to define more rigorously and clearly the transition from logical design to physical design
- to focus on the design of interactive systems by providing a dialogue design technique integrated with a formal approach to process specification
- to ensure that support tools for the method could be developed more easily
- to facilitate developments of the method in the future.

3.2 Key features of SSADM Version 4

SSADM Version 4 has a modular structure but still retains the same number of stages. Figure 1 overleaf shows Version 4 and Version 3 together. The key features of Version 4 are:

- it has a modular structure around key management decision points (section 3.2.1)
- the method is product driven (what is to be produced is fully defined, so what to develop and when is known) and *products* have quality criteria (see section 3.2.2)
- there is now greater formality in logical design, offering portability to different physical environments (see section 3.2.3)
- the physical design module is now more customisable (see section 3.2.3)
- activities that interface with SSADM – project, quality and infrastructure management – are fully described in the SSADM Version 4 reference manual (see section 3.2.4)

Migrating from SSADM Version 3 to Version 4

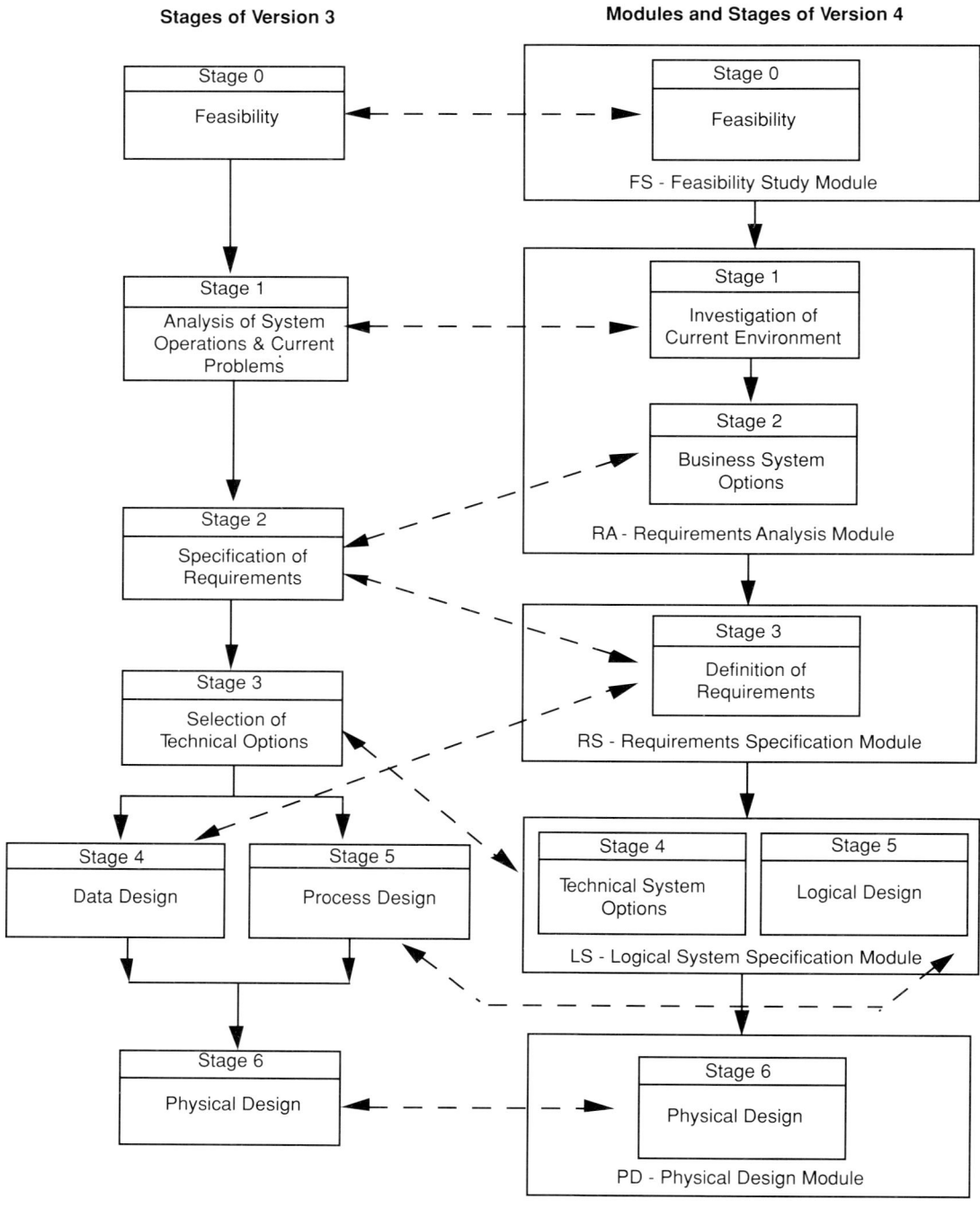

Figure 1: SSADM Version 3 and Version 4 compared

- information flows to project management are better documented with the introduction of the Information Highway (section 3.2.1)
- a new technique, function definition, enhances the three views of requirement (section 3.3.2)
- more emphasis on users and dialogue design issues (section 3.3.3).

3.2.1 Modular structure

The modular structure of SSADM Version 4 means that each unit of SSADM activity, Module, Stage and Step, can be thought of as a 'black box'. Each box has a set of inputs, activities within the box and outputs. The inputs and outputs are both comprised of products. The activities within the box either amend these input products or use them to create new products; these then flow from the box as outputs.

As a result of its modular structure, Version 4 is easier to understand and to teach. There is now a set of high level concepts that are easy to assimilate by people new to the method. Customisation of the method is easier as the model is based on a product driven approach. It is therefore relatively easy to trace the impact of not producing a product and where gaps left by missing products need to be filled.

The information highway

SSADM Version 4 has been designed to promote the exchange of information from the SSADM activity to project management via the information highway, as shown in Figure 2 overleaf. This highway is a concept that shows all output products from a Stage flowing along it until they are passed as inputs to the next Stage. Similarly all communication from the management of the SSADM project flow along the highway and thence into a Stage. Reports back to project management also use the highway.

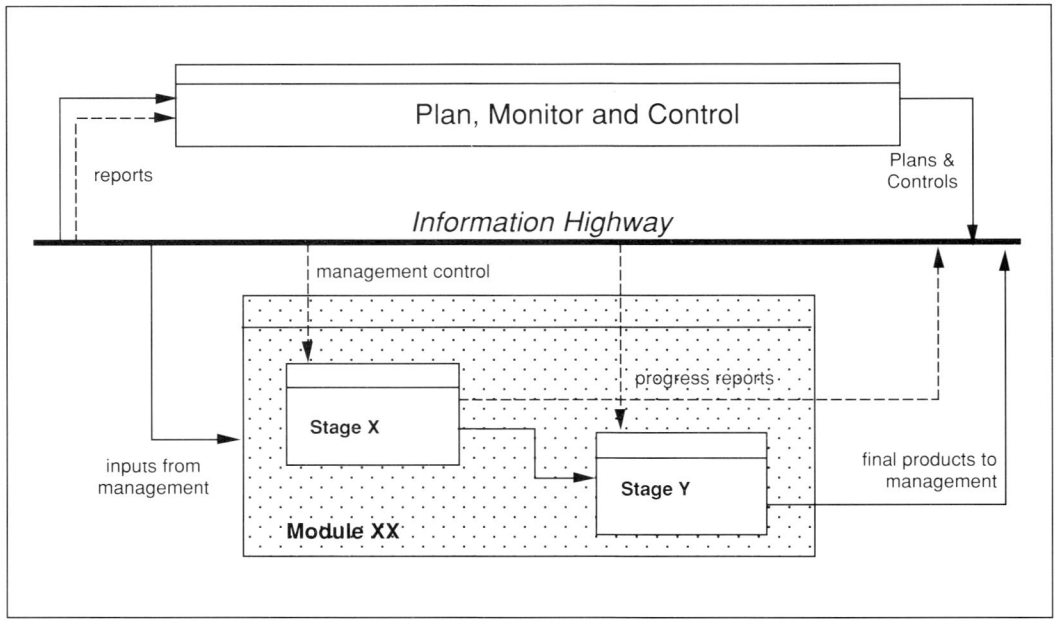

Figure 2: The information highway

3.2.2	Product driven approach	An integral part of the modularity of SSADM Version 4 is the product driven approach it uses, with products described in PRINCE terms. This approach focuses on what is to be produced and not on the activities that are to be undertaken, as did Version 3. Products are much easier to define precisely than are activities. SSADM products are defined in the Product Breakdown Structure (PBS). A PBS shows product relationships; it contains a Product Description for each product (this covers derivation, content and quality criteria for the product) and also shows if the product is itself comprised of other products. This ensures that a very clear idea is obtained of the composition of all products, and where they are created and used.
3.2.3	Portability of logical design	Logical Design (Stage 5) and Physical Design (Stage 6) have been completely separated in SSADM Version 4. Logical design is now one integrated stage that facilitates portability of the logical system design. This ensures that no implementation or developmental constraints are imposed on the system until a decision has been made about the implementation environment by project management. The SSADM Design Authority Board encourages suppliers to produce tool specific guides describing how their product interfaces with SSADM.

Chapter 3
Technical overview of SSADM Version 4

3.2.4 SSADM interfaces

There are activities which must, or may, be carried out during the life of a project using SSADM which are not covered by SSADM. Some of these activities are referred to in the Version 4 manual under the title Project Procedures and include:

- project management
- quality assurance
- risk assessment and planning
- testing.

3.3 New and changed techniques

3.3.1 Overview

The names and contents of stages have changed as new techniques have been added, other techniques have been improved and the exploitation of some techniques has changed position within the method.

FS Feasibility Study Module	Stage 0 Feasibility
RA Requirements Analysis Module	Stage 1 Investigation of Current Environment
	Stage 2 Business System Options
RS Requirements Specification Module	Stage 3 Definition of Requirements
LS Logical System Specification Module	Stage 4 Technical System Options
	Stage 5 Logical Design
PD Physical Design Module	Stage 6 Physical Design

3.3.2 New techniques

Several new techniques have been added to the method:

- **requirements definition** – the emphasis has been firmly placed on eliciting requirements with the introduction of this technique. It deals with security, audit and other non-functional aspects of the system as well as the functional requirements (see section 3.4.1)

- **function definition** – this is a clear view of the processing requirements for a user of the system wishing to undertake a task in response to a business event. It provides a systematic transformation of the data flow diagram in early analysis to the formal process specification and provides user oriented packaging of processing requirements from specification to logical and physical design (see section 3.4.3)

- **specification prototyping** – this is a technique that has been introduced to use support tools to animate the results of analysis. The technique helps to validate the analyst's interpretation of the users' requirements *and* the users' understanding of what is really required (see section 3.4.3)

- **effect correspondence diagramming** – this, combined with entity life history analysis, gives the Entity/Event model of the requirement for system processing (see section 3.4.3)

3.3.3 Changed techniques

Several techniques familiar to Version 3 practitioners have changed in Version 4. These are:

- **dialogue design** – this identifies users and their roles in relation to the information system that is being designed, then matches these against functions to produce logical dialogues for both batch and on-line processing (see section 3.4.5)

- **logical database process design** – a diagrammatic notation is now used in both update and enquiry processing for improved understanding and presentation in preference to the textual documents that were used in Version 3 (see section 3.4.6)

- **physical design** – Version 4 provides a template of physical design activities, which must be tailored to suit the implementation environment (see section 3.4.6)

3.3.4 Moved techniques

Two techniques have been moved within the method to make them more effective. The moved techniques are:

- **Business System Options** – this has now become a Stage, like Technical System Options (Technical Options in Version 3), to highlight the importance of the decisions that need to be made on business requirements after the end of the Stage.

- **Relational Data Analysis** – this has been moved forward in the method so that it takes place before the Entity Life History work. This means that Entity/Event Modelling work takes place on a stable Logical Data Model in Version 4. In Version 3 Relational Data Analysis often caused changes to the data model that meant rework of the Entity Life Histories, and consequent waste of effort by practitioners.

3.4 Changes to the method

The main changes are as follows.

3.4.1 Stage 1 - Investigation of the Current Environment

In Version 3 Stage 1 was an investigation of the current system, producing current DFDs, a Logical Data Model and a Problems Requirements List. In Version 4 Stage 1 still investigates the current environment, but this investigation is aimed at gathering requirements. There is a new technique, Requirements Definition, to assist in this process. Requirements are documented in the Requirements Catalogue, with attention being directed at not only what has to be done but also at how well it has to be done. The *how well* aspects are documented as Service Level Requirements attached to requirements. The current environment is still modelled using the data flow modelling and logical data modelling techniques.

3.4.2 Stage 2 - Business System Options

The profile of Business System Options (BSOs) has been raised to match that of Technical System Options. The selection of a BSO is a major decision point in the development of the new system and this is reflected in Stage 2 being wholly devoted to the creation and selection of BSOs.

3.4.3 Stage 3 - Definition of Requirements

In Version 3 Stage 2 covered BSOs and the specification of requirements. In Version 4 BSOs have a stage to themselves with Stage 3 being devoted to requirements specification. Required System DFDs are still developed as is the Required System Logical Data Model. Enquiry Access Paths are produced for functions with enquiry elements. Throughout Stage 3 requirements definition is used to capture requirements in the Requirements Catalogue.

There is a new technique, *function definition*, which provides the user view of the system processing and creates a bridge between the two process specification techniques of data flow diagramming and entity-event modelling. I/O Structures are created during function definition and are then input to relational data analysis and to dialogue design.

Relational data analysis (RDA) now takes place before entity-event modelling and is used to enhance the Required System LDM.

Another new technique, *specification prototyping*, has been included in Stage 3 to assist in the validation of requirements. This technique is used to identify errors or omissions in the requirements specification and may also generate presentational requirements for the user interface.

In Version 4 the processing needed to respond to an event entering the system is specified more formally than in Version 3. In Stage 3 a new sub-technique, *effect correspondence diagramming*, takes the results of ELH analysis and produces, for each event, a diagrammatic structure showing the correspondence between the effects of that event. In Stage 5 the Effect Correspondence Diagrams are developed into process structures. The technique encompassing ELH analysis and effect correspondence diagramming is called *entity-event modelling*.

In Version 4 there is a replacement technique for *dialogue design*. The technique is used initially in Stage 1 to identify users and their roles, and also in Step 330, where dialogues are identified. Most of dialogue design takes place in Stage 5.

The *system objectives* are confirmed as part of the specification of requirements. Service level requirements are documented against requirements in the Requirements Catalogue and against functions on the Function Definitions earlier in the method, but there is a final check in Stage 3 that the non-functional requirements have been fully documented.

Chapter 3
Technical overview of SSADM Version 4

3.4.4	Stage 4 - Technical System Options	This stage is equivalent to Version 3 Stage 3. Technical System Options are created and an option selected. This stage is carried out in parallel with Stage 5 with no interaction between the two stages. Stage 4 in Version 3 contained data design. This included carrying out relational data analysis and the subsequent creation of the Composite Logical Data Design. As described above RDA and the subsequent updating of the data model is now carried out in Stage 3.
3.4.5	Stage 5 - Logical Design	This stage contains *logical database process design* and *dialogue design*. In this stage further detail is added to the processing specifications passed from Stage 3. The Enquiry Access Paths are developed into Enquiry Process Models. The Effect Correspondence Diagrams are transformed into Update Process Models. These logical process models are diagrammatic structures and replace Logical Enquiry Process Outlines and Logical Update Process Outlines. With the introduction of ECDs and logical process models there is now a well defined route through from ELH analysis to program specification.
		Most of dialogue design is still carried out in Stage 5.
3.4.6	Stage 6 - Physical Design	Physical design in Version 4, as in Version 3, is carried out in Stage 6. However Version 4 acknowledges the problem of giving physical data and process design guidance for a wide variety of implementation environments. Thus Version 4 gives a template structure and general principles for physical design. Physical designers with a detailed knowledge of the target environment must tailor the general structure and principles to suit that environment.
3.5	**SSADM Version 4 documentation**	Version 4 is documented in a reference manual, published as a four volume set by NCC (see Bibliography).
	SSADM Version 4 Reference Manual	The four volumes are:

- Volume 1 – containing the SSADM philosophy and concepts, the foundation techniques, such as requirements definition and the Feasibility Module

- Volume 2 – documenting the Requirements Analysis and Requirements Specification Modules

13

Migrating from SSADM Version 3 to Version 4

- Volume 3 – covering the Logical System Specification and Physical Design Modules
- Volume 4 – containing the Dictionary, which fully documents the products, and the glossary of terms.

Information Systems Engineering Library volumes

CCTA produced subject guides for SSADM Version 3 which described how other methods or techniques interfaced with SSADM. The existing guides are being updated for Version 4 and new titles are in preparation. These will be published as volumes in the Information Systems Engineering Library.

Physical Design product-specific guides

Stage 6 in Version 4 provides example activities based on general principles which designers can adapt to produce project specific and implementation environment specific Stage 6 Activity Descriptions. The SSADM Design Authority Board encourages suppliers to produce product-specific guides detailing how SSADM can be tailored for use with their particular products.

4 Issues to be considered before migration

There are some key issues which must be considered before planning the migration to SSADM Version 4. (Chapters 5 and 6 cover migration itself). These issues include:

- ease and effectiveness of systems analysis and design in the delivery of systems
- the benefits, costs and opportunities of migration
- effective planning for migration
- project management considerations for Version 4 projects, such as project planning and project control
- Version 4 training and skills requirements
- availability of support, such as training, CASE tools and consultancy
- conformance to policies described in the organisation's IS strategy
- maintenance of Version 3 systems in a Version 4 environment.

These issues are discussed below.

4.1 Effective delivery of systems

An information system must be designed to meet business needs. The requirements catalogue in SSADM Version 4 is used to document and update business requirements. This ensures that these requirements are addressed and delivered – not diluted or diverted by a series of local operational requirements.

Quality costs money. SSADM Version 4 sets out quality criteria so that systems are designed to meet only those objectives that are required, without risk of over-engineering.

4.2 Benefits, costs and opportunities

Migration to Version 4 allows managers to retain and build on existing investment, but this has to be balanced against the costs of migration.

Benefits

Improved interfaces to project management ensure that business objectives are supported throughout a project, without the risk of decisions being made at the wrong level or by the wrong people on a project using SSADM.

Prototyping can be effectively carried out – because it is an integral part of the method and is fed directly into the products, effort is not wasted. SSADM Version 4 is more rigorous and flexible, making it easier to tailor the method to suit managers' or projects' particular needs. Improved rigour makes software re-use easier to plan and achieve.

Deliverables (including quality) can now be tightly defined and are more comprehensible. This is especially important for turnkey development, as there is now better understanding and control of the deliverables.

Costs

The major costs of migration are those of conversion training (covered in section 4.5) and of migrating to a new environment with an existing portfolio of projects. These costs will depend on the extent of existing investment and the scale of projects under development.

Opportunities

Migration to Version 4 provides a baseline on which to build for future developments. The method can now address prototyping and distributed systems, with the advantages of an integrated project support environment and earlier established relationships to IS strategy and strategic planning.

There is also the opportunity to seriously review the current programme of work in the project portfolio before committing any project to development in a new environment.

4.3 Effective planning for migration

Effective planning minimises the disruption to an organisation during the transition from one environment to another. Migration planning is discussed in Chapter 5. There may be advantages of migrating individual projects at a specific point in development; Chapter 6 covers this topic in detail.

Chapter 4
Issues to be considered before migration

4.4 **Project management considerations**

SSADM, like any other structured method, can only work effectively when used in conjunction with a project management method. Version 4 of SSADM has been designed to be used with PRINCE (PRojects IN Controlled Environments), but has the characteristics necessary for use with any good product-based project management method.

These characteristics include well-defined activities and products, with built-in review and decision points in the method. The information highway on the structural model is of crucial importance to project management (shown in Figure 2 on page 8). All products passing to or from SSADM do so via the information highway and nothing can appear on the highway without having met the project management method quality requirements. All traffic on the highway is predetermined, predefined and preplanned.

Project planning

SSADM is designed to be flexible. Thus the SSADM structural model and product descriptions can be viewed as templates which can be tailored to suit a particular project's needs. Tailoring may take place depending on a number of criteria, for example:

- the size and complexity of the project
- the number and experience of project staff, including users
- the type of project, for example the balance between retrieval and update processing, or the ratio of on-line to off-line processing
- the CASE tool or tools in use
- the point at which the target implementation environment is known
- the ability to prototype
- whether it is a turnkey or in-house development
- project and organisation standards.

17

Migrating from SSADM Version 3 to Version 4

Planning points

At the beginning of each module the activities to be performed during that module need to be examined and the plans conformed. Three major points where SSADM planning activities are performed are:

- Step 010, Prepare for the Feasibility Study
- Step 110, Establish Analysis Framework
- Step 610, Prepare for Physical Design.

Although detailed planning and estimating takes place within the province of the project management method it is within these steps that the SSADM activities and products for the project are specified. The products of these steps include an Activity Network, Activity Descriptions, the Product Breakdown Structure (PBS) and Product Descriptions. The Dictionary section of the reference manual gives templates for SSADM Version 4 PBS and Product Descriptions. The Structural Model elements of the manual give the standard Activity Descriptions and provide the basis from which the Activity Network can be derived.

Above the information highway on the SSADM Structural Model diagrams is the Plan, Monitor and Control process. This is shown explicitly on the SSADM lifecycle diagram, but is implicit in all the Structural Model diagrams. This process can be decomposed to illustrate the interface between SSADM Version 4 and the project management procedures. Other methods (SDM, CRAMM, function point analysis etc) that need to interface with SSADM should also be considered so that their interfaces may be amended if necessary.

Project control

Projects using SSADM are launched by the issuing of a Project Initiation Document. In Steps 010 and 110, project control is exercised as this document is reviewed to ensure it contains sufficient information for the project to proceed. This is particularly important at the end of Feasibility, when a decision is made on whether to proceed with the project or not.

The modular structure of SSADM allows control to be exercised at the end of each module. Approval can be given for the work carried out so far and authority granted for the next Module to proceed. This is

Chapter 4
Issues to be considered before migration

particularly important at the end of Feasibility, when a decision is made on whether to proceed with the project or not.

There are built-in decision points within the SSADM structure. These appear in Stage 0, where feasibility options are created; Stage 2 where Business System Options are developed; and Stage 4 where Technical System Options are constructed. At each of these points options are passed to the Project Board with supporting Impact and Cost/Benefit Analyses. Thus the Project Board can influence the direction of the project or decide the project is no longer viable.

Quality control

Each Stage ends with a Step which assembles the SSADM products and reviews them for correctness and consistency. At the end of each module the products are passed to the information highway so that the project management method can input them to the formal review process. Each product has quality criteria specified in its Product Description.

Estimating

The more rigorous specification of activities and products in Version 4 will facilitate estimating.

4.5 Version 4 training

An SSADM Version 4 training course accreditation scheme exists, with several training providers already accredited to give full SSADM Version 4 training. A list of these organisations can be obtained from the SSADM Certificate Board of the ISEB.

Different types of SSADM training are required for different roles in the project:

- *project managers* will require a an overview of Version 4 with project management implications highlighted. Training providers offer one day management seminars

- *team leaders* need a full understanding of Version 4, with the changes in Version 4, including structural model and technique changes highlighted, and an understanding of the impact of the changes on project support facilities

- *analysts/designers with Version 3 experience* require an in-depth understanding of the new techniques, an appreciation of the structural model and an understanding of the impact on support facilities

Migrating from SSADM Version 3 to Version 4

- *analysts/designers with no SSADM experience* require full SSADM Version 4 training
- *people new to analysis and design* require basic systems training plus full SSADM Version 4 training
- *users* will need training to understand the Version 4 activities and products.

Full SSADM training	The IS Examination Board (ISEB) has stipulated that a minimum of 80 hours is required to cover the full SSADM syllabus. The SSADM Certificate is to be split into two qualifications: the first covering analysis, the second design. Training providers can offer courses in either analysis or design or both.
Conversion training	Accredited training organisations can offer conversion courses for SSADM Version 3 practitioners. The aim of these conversion courses is to teach delegates the differences between Version 3 and Version 4. Conversion courses should be at least 25 hours long to cover the differences adequately. Organisations should look carefully at their objectives in seeking conversion training. 25 hours is long enough to highlight the developments in Version 4 but may not adequately prepare practitioners to use the new techniques.
Project management training	Project management courses are widely available. An accreditation scheme for PRINCE trainers is in the process of being set up.

4.6 Version 4 skills

Summarised below are the skills required to carry out an SSADM Version 4 development project. Clearly more than one of these skills may be found in any particular individual, but the identification of the skills necessary at different points in the method assists the project planner to allocate resources to the project and the project manager to identify training needs. Figure 3 shows the SSADM Version 4 Modules and Stages.

Project management skills	Project management activities are outside the boundary of SSADM (they are fully documented in PRINCE). If a decision is taken to migrate to Version 4 during a project's life (see section 6.9) it may be prudent to consider the migration as a distinct project stage, and consider whether any specific technical skills will be needed by the manager of this stage.

Chapter 4
Issues to be considered before migration

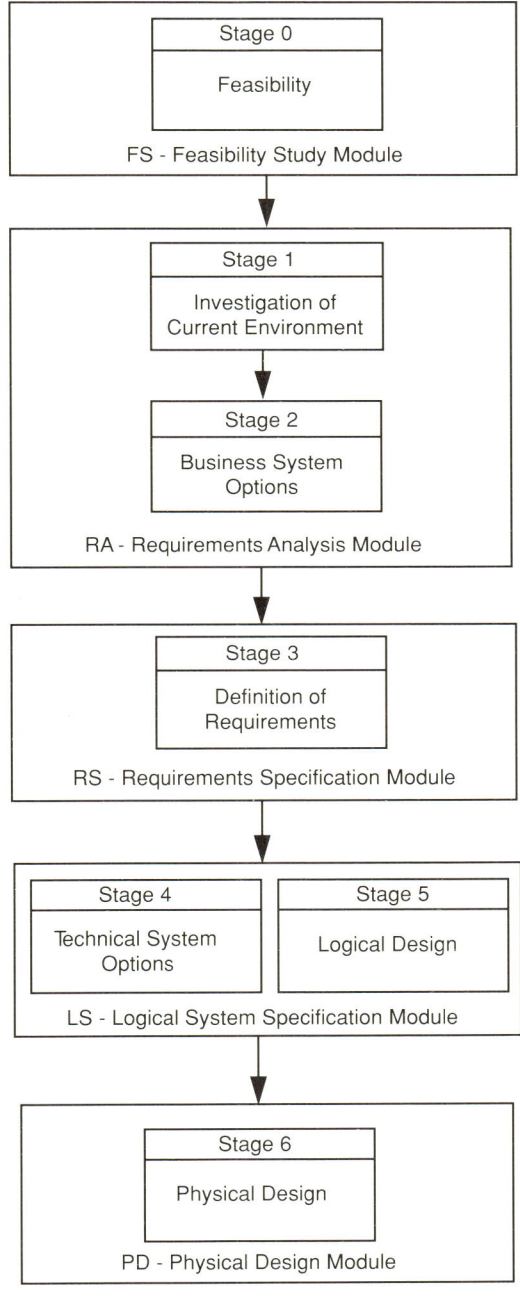

Figure 3: SSADM Version 4 Modules and Stages

The project board may implement different management structures, depending on the resources required and the skills available, such as:

- one project manager, supported by a module manager for each module
- one project manager who also assumes the role of module manager throughout
- a succession of module managers, each assuming the role of project manager for the duration of the project.

Requirements analysis skills

Listed below are the requirements analysis skills needed during an SSADM project and the Version 4 modules where they are used:

- Feasibility, Requirements Analysis and Requirements Specification Modules
  - interviewing
  - information gathering
  - inter-personal communication
  - requirements definition.

Data modelling skills

Listed below are the data modelling skills needed during an SSADM project and the Version 4 modules where they are used:

- Feasibility Module and Requirements Analysis Module
  - logical data modelling
- Requirements Specification Module
  - logical data modelling
  - relational data analysis
  - ELH analysis and effect correspondence diagramming
- Logical System Specification Module
  - physical data design
  - environment-specific data design

Chapter 4
Issues to be considered before migration

- Physical Design Module
  - logical data modelling
  - physical data design
  - environment-specific data design.

Process modelling skills   Listed below are the data modelling skills needed during an SSADM project and the Version 4 modules where they are used:

- Feasibility Module and Requirements Analysis Module
  - data flow diagramming
- Requirements Specification Module
  - data flow diagramming
  - function definition
  - specification prototyping knowledge
- Logical System Specification Module
  - physical process specification
  - function definition
  - dialogue design
  - logical database process design
- Physical Design Module
  - function definition
  - physical process specification
  - environment-specific process specification.

Additional specialist skills required   Other specialist skills and knowledge that are required during an SSADM development include:

- capacity planning
- human factors, ergonomics
- security
- data communications
- database administration
- data administration.

4.7 Project support
CASE tools

It is assumed that projects using SSADM Version 4 will make use of IT support. For Version 3 a CASE tool conformance scheme was set up to help both users and suppliers of CASE tools. This scheme rates tools on a four star conformance scale.

CCTA aims to make the Version 4 scheme more flexible. The objective is to classify tools according to their strengths allowing a prospective buyer of a CASE tool to set out his requirements for an SSADM tool and match it to the tool that best meets those requirements. The SSADM Design Authority Board is encouraging a competitive and differentiated CASE tool market.

The SSADM Users Group tools sub-group carried out appraisals of some Version 3 tools. Appraisals will be carried out on Version 4 tools as they appear on the market.

For projects moving from Version 3 to 4 (especially in mid-project) consider how much support is given in converting Version 3 products to Version 4 standards when deciding on a Version 4 CASE tool. For example, many of the changes in logical data modelling are notational.

Consultancy support

There are a number of consultancy organisations that are well-placed to provide Version 4 support.

4.8 Standards

There is a whole range of standards which could impact on a project using SSADM including installation standards, organisational standards, methodology standards (for example PRINCE) and programming and design standards. Standards which constrain an SSADM project may be documented in the project Terms of Reference in the Project Initiation Document or may be incorporated in the SSADM documentation as the project progresses.

Version 4 has a well-defined set of products. These products are defined in the Product Breakdown Structure in Volume 4 of the SSADM Reference Manual. The Product Descriptions, in the Product Breakdown Structure, provide a standard model for each product. These products may have to be tailored to meet the needs or standards of a particular project or of a particular installation.

Chapter 4
Issues to be considered before migration

The format of products given in the reference manual is only suggested. It is the *information content* that is important. Therefore forms may be designed for specific projects or a CASE tool may be used which holds and outputs the information in a different way.

The requirement to conform to a particular standard may be recorded in the Requirements Catalogue. In Steps 420 and 610 the Application Development Standards are documented.This contains the Application Style Guide, which is developed from the Installation Style Guide and documents standards for the user environment; the Application Naming Standards; the Physical Design Strategy and the Physical Environment Classification.

4.9 SSADM Version 3 maintenance

There should be no difficulty in maintaining Version 3 projects in a Version 4 environment, as SSADM Version 4 builds on familiar tools and techniques. However, this may be a suitable time to consider market testing for outsourcing of Version 3-supported projects or for conversion of existing documentation.

Managers need to consider these issues in deciding on the most appropriate option for Version 3 maintenance:

- how long is the application likely to be needed?
- how much change is expected?
- what is the anticipated scale of change?

5 Developing a migration plan for the organisation

The move to Version 4 needs careful planning because it may have an effect at several planning levels of an organisation:

- *IS strategy planning*
  management and technical policies, including standards

- *tactical planning*
  project portfolio; human resource planning

- *project planning*
  systems development and maintenance.

The migration should be managed as a project in its own right with a migration plan for the organisation as a whole and for each project. An impact analysis should be carried out for each proposed migration project. If more than one project is migrating to Version 4 there should be a person whose role is to co-ordinate the migration across projects. For each project there should also be a person who is responsible for reporting back to the co-ordinator.

The migration must be carefully monitored and the plan adjusted to take account of experience gained. Above all, everyone should be kept informed.

In developing the organisation's migration plan managers must consider where they are now, where they want to be and how to get there. These topics are discussed in more detail below.

5.1 Where you are now

Managers must assess their present position including:

- the types of projects that are undertaken

- the maintenance load

- the type of staff that they have, including their skill levels, their potential, their career development

- the training and human resource development policies that are in place

- the IS infrastructure, including:
  - the IS strategy

- other methods and techniques in use, such as strategy planning and capacity planning

- the CASE tools already in use and the investment in the equipment on which they run

- standards, for example conformance to ISO 9000 and standard change control procedures.

5.2 Where do you want to be?

Managers must be aware of what they are aiming at, including:

- the types of service provider to be used, for example policies on turnkey projects and buying-in consultants and contractors

- the types of application or system which will be in place

- the types of implementation environment under which applications/systems will run

- the types of project to be undertaken in future

- methods of working which will be used in future

- the future workload.

5.3 How to get there

Given a good understanding of where you are now and where you want to be in the future, managers must develop a plan for how to get there, including:

- planning training to ensure that the right skills are available at the right time

- identifying consultancy support requirements and making the most effective use of that support

- identifying the impact of migration on CASE tools

- identifying the impact of CASE tools on migration

- co-ordinating the concurrent use of two versions of the SSADM for example maintaining two sets of standards

- identifying the impact of the use of application generators/4GLs on adopting Version 4

- assessing the impact of migration on project procedures, such as project management, capacity planning, configuration management.

6 Migration of SSADM projects

6.1 Approaches to migrating the organisation's projects to SSADM Version 4

There are advantages and disadvantages to each of the approaches of moving to Version 4. No hard and fast rules are given as there are many variables involved, including:

- the number of current SSADM projects
- the interdependencies between projects
- the rate that new projects are initiated
- the timescales of projects, both new ones and those already under way
- the types of project being undertaken
- the budgets available for training and CASE tool support
- the availability of staff.

The approaches to migrating the current portfolio of projects to Version 4 can be integrated with adopting Version 4 on individual projects. Managers must assess their own situation and decide the best way to migrate.

Some of the options for migrating the organisation to Version 4 with their associated advantages and disadvantages are listed below.

6.2 Project by project basis

In this option projects which would gain the most significant benefits from the use of Version 4 are identified. These projects may be new projects or ones already under way using Version 3. These projects should be placed in a priority order for migration (see the IS Planning Subject Guide *Prioritisation* for further information about prioritisation of IS projects.). One project may be identified as the pilot for Version 4. The pilot project should be one that is seen as being relatively straightforward and carrying little risk.

The pilot project is used to gain experience with techniques and project management for Version 4. As experience is gained in Version 4 the other projects identified for migration can proceed. As with all plans the migration plan should be monitored and amended in the light of new knowledge.

Advantages:

- this option carries the least risk as early problems can be ironed out on one project
- there is less initial investment in training
- later projects can benefit from practitioner skills gained on the first Version 4 project
- each project is assessed for the benefit to be gained from Version 4.

Disadvantages:

- dual standards have to be maintained
- staff may have to understand both versions
- different CASE tools are needed.

6.3 All new projects move to Version 4

With this option only new projects move to Version 4, whilst existing projects are completed using Version 3. This option may be suitable for organisations which have many projects and want to cut down the number of possible migration projects.

Advantages:

- this option results in the least amount of rework and redocumentation
- training of staff can be staggered to coincide with new projects
- later projects can benefit from practitioner skills gained on the first Version 4 projects
- full benefits of Version 4 are realised for each new project.

Disadvantages:

- projects already underway do not benefit from the Version 4 improvements
- dual standards have to be maintained
- staff may have to understand both versions
- different CASE tools are needed.

6.4 All projects migrate to Version 4 at once (big bang approach)

In this option all projects, new ones and ones underway migrate to Version 4 at once. This is the riskiest of the options as there is no opportunity to learn on one project and apply the lessons learned.

Advantages:

- no need to maintain two sets of standards
- all projects can use the same CASE tool
- interfaces between projects will be less of a problem.

Disadvantages:

- there will be additional work to migrate existing projects
- time-critical projects may be delayed
- early problems with the method may have to be ironed out on all projects
- there will need to be a large investment in training in a short time
- it is difficult to find the 'right time' to migrate
- no opportunity to test out project estimating guidelines.

This option is not recommended unless there are only a small number of projects, all of which would benefit significantly from Version 4.

6.5 Choosing projects for migration

The projects chosen to be the first to be developed wholly using Version 4 or those chosen to migrate to Version 4 during the project lifecycle should be those which would gain maximum benefit from Version 4. There are many factors which will influence how much benefit is gained by moving to Version 4. These include:

- the experience of the development staff
- the stage of development the project has reached. The earlier in the project life migration takes place the greater the benefits to be gained and the lower the project migration costs.

- the availability of support, such as training, consultancy and CASE tools
- management commitment
- the relative importance of quality as opposed to timescales
- the type of project.

  Certain types of project will benefit more from Version 4 than others, for example:
  - larger projects will see more benefit in return for the conversion effort than smaller ones
  - projects whose success is critical to the business will benefit more from the improved rigour of Version 4
  - projects with a high proportion of on-line activity will gain from the improved dialogue design technique and the new specification prototyping technique of Version 4
  - projects with complex processing will benefit from the more rigorous process design techniques of Version 4
  - large database update systems will gain from the improved process analysis, design and specification techniques
  - projects with a high proportion of enquiries will benefit from the new enquiry process modelling techniques.

However, it is safer to choose small low-risk projects as the first projects to migrate. Any early problems can then be overcome with the least risk to the business.

Consideration should be given to providing an environment where SSADM Version 4 can prove itself. A low-risk project is a safe option for trying out Version 4, but such a project may not provide the opportunity to demonstrate the range and strengths of Version 4. There is a need to balance the options of low-risk opportunity to prove Version 4 to decide which projects are most suitable.

Chapter 6
Migration of SSADM projects

6.6 Adopting Version 4 on individual projects

Obviously the simplest and safest place to migrate to Version 4 is at the start of a project. However, many SSADM projects have long timescales and it would be a pity not to take advantage of the benefits offered by Version 4 if it would be beneficial to the project. Each project must be considered in turn to determine the benefits to be gained from Version 4. The benefits should be balanced against the likely delay, disruption or problems that converting to Version 4 during the project's life could cause. Below are some suggestions for how or where Version 4 could be adopted during a project's life.

6.7 Adopting new Version 4 techniques within a Version 3 structure

Version 4 can be adopted mid-way through a Version 3 project by using some of the new techniques to augment Version 3. The techniques adopted depend on the type of project and the stage the development has reached, so hard and fast rules cannot be given. Some examples are listed below:

- where the human computer interface is important to the success of the project, specification prototyping could be carried out to ensure the requirements in this area have been correctly and fully documented

- the function definition technique may be used to identify and specify functions as Version 3 did not explain how to identify functions

- it may be preferable to adopt the Version 4 dialogue design technique for a project

- the Version 4 Effect Correspondence Diagrams and Enquiry Access Paths could be developed and input to the logical database design technique to bridge the gap between logical and physical design identified in Version 3 (operations would have to be added to the ELHs).

The advantages of adopting Version 4 techniques within the Version 3 structure are:

- members of the team do not have to learn and use a whole range of new techniques and a new structure all at once

- the project is not held up unnecessarily by the need to replan and redocument for Version 4
- an assessment is made of which Version 4 techniques will provide the greatest benefit to a particular project.

The disadvantages are:

- it may be difficult to find tailored training
- there will be a certain amount of extra work needed to specify how to use the Version 4 techniques in the Version 3 structure and to interface them to Version 3 techniques
- two tools may be needed to support the project if the tool in use cannot support both Version 3 and 4 simultaneously. There would be some additional work necessary to interface the products from the two tools.

There are any number of permutations for importing Version 4 techniques into the Version 3 structure depending on circumstances. Organisations must consider their own circumstances and those of individual projects.

6.8 Using elements of the Version 4 structure with Version 3 techniques

It is possible to use elements of the Version 4 Structure within a Version 3 project. For example:

- a Version 3 project may bring the RDA technique forward into Stage 3 so that the Logical Data Structure is updated with the RDA results before ELH analysis takes place
- projects may use the product descriptions in the Version 4 Dictionary and apply them, albeit in a modified form, to the comparable Version 3 products
- the Version 4 template of physical design activities may be used on a Version 3 project
- the modularity of Version 4 could be imposed on a Version 3 project. Although this would require some reworking to define the module products, there would be the benefit of explicit break points where a defined product is passed to management for approval

Chapter 6
Migration of SSADM projects

- the concept of carrying out TSOs in parallel with logical design may be adopted, if resources are available, to shorten a project's timescale.

The advantages of this approach are:

- there is less risk as staff can gradually become accustomed to Version 4

- an assessment is made as to which elements of the Version 4 structure will provide the greatest benefit to a particular project

- there is an opportunity to take advantage of some of the Version 4 improvements even if there is insufficient budget for full Version 4 training.

The disadvantages are:

- the full benefit of Version 4 is not realised

- there will be a certain amount of extra work needed to specify how to integrate the chosen Version 4 elements with the Version 3 techniques and structure

- the full migration to Version 4 will be delayed and staff will have to learn two new versions of the method, a hybrid of Version 3 and 4 and then the full Version 4.

6.9 Adopting Version 4 during a project's life (cut-over points)

For some projects, especially those with a long timescale or those which can get most benefit from the Version 4 improvements, it is worthwhile considering migrating to Version 4 during the life of the project. Described below are the cut-over points where this move could be made.

Where cut-over points are described the general principle is not to go back and update the Version 3 products where they are deficient but to add the information to the appropriate Version 4 product. For example when migrating to Version 4 at the beginning of the Requirements Specification Module the Logical Data Structure will need to be updated with Version 4 notation. The changes should not be made to the Version 3 product but to the Version 4 Required System LDM.

However, this principle needs qualification when a project is being cut over from Version 3 to Version 4 and considering contracting out the work of the next module to a third party. The modular nature of Version 4, with well-defined products from each module, means that project managers can contract out the work for a particular module. They need to consider how the re-documentation is to be effected when deciding whether or not to contract-out work. There are two options for carrying out the necessary rework:

- the project team bring the Version 3 documentation to Version 4 standard themselves before the contract is let

- the required rework of Version 3 documentation is tightly defined, becoming part of the contract and thus the responsibility of the third party.

If these options are not feasible a decision should be taken not to contract out the work.

When making a decision on migrating to Version 4 during the life of a project a factor to consider is not just how much rework is required, but how far the CASE tool supports that rework. If different tools are used for the two versions there will be some effort in transferring or re-inputting the documentation from the Version 3 tool to the Version 4 tool. Another factor to consider is the availability and cost of the Version 4 tools.

Below are the suggested cut-over points, together with a summary of the impact of migration and its advantages. Annex A gives further detail of the redocumentation necessary at each cut-over point, except for cut-over point 6. Figure 4 illustrates the six suggested cut-over points.

Cut-over point 1

From the end of the Version 3 Feasibility Study to the beginning of Version 4 Requirements Analysis Module the Feasability Study is undertaken as a separate project.

Migrating from Version 3 to Version 4 of SSADM at the end of a Version 3 Feasibility Study is relatively straightforward.This equates to the project starting in Version 4 at the beginning of Requirements Analysis Module (RA) . A Feasibility Study will usually have taken place at this point in both versions of the method. The aim of the study is to determine whether the proposed information system can meet the business needs and whether a the investment needed to produce the system is justified.

Chapter 6
Migration of SSADM projects

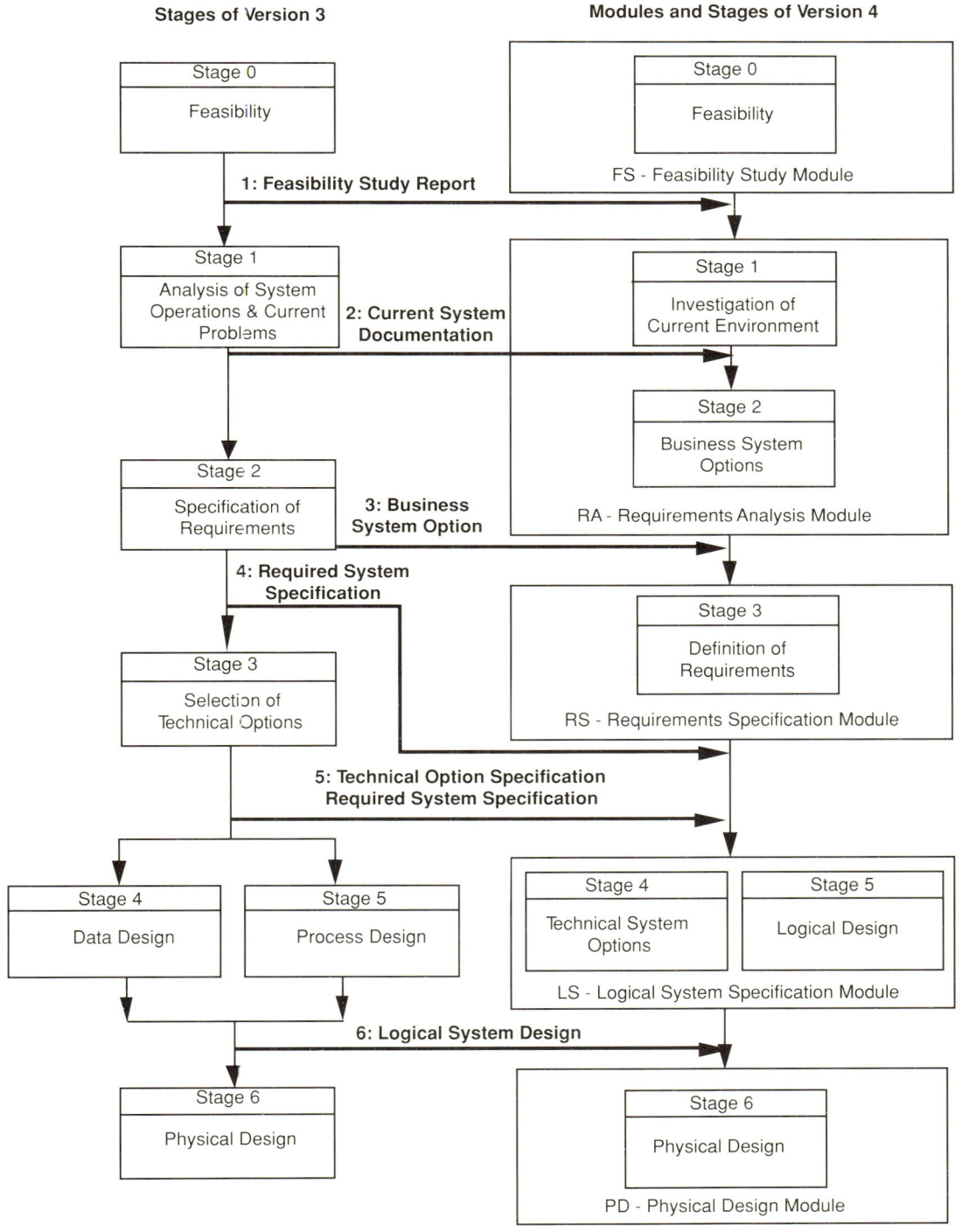

Figure 4: Version 3 to Version 4 cut-over points

Some additional work may need to be carried out if a Version 3 Feasibility Study is carried out rather than a Version 4 study, but this should not be significant. Version 4 does not assume that all Version 4 projects should begin with a Version 4 Feasibility Study. It is recognised that other methods, for example soft systems, could be used to carry out the preliminary study. Carrying out a Version 3 Feasibility Study should not be a problem. The additional work required is described in more detail in Annex A.

The advantages of migrating at this point are:

- there is a very clear separation between the Feasibility Module and the Requirements Analysis Module in Version 4

- there is the minimum of SSADM documentation in existence at this point and the documentation that is available is easy to convert to Version 4 standard

- most of the benefits of using Version 4 can be gained.

Cut-over point 2   *From the end of Version 3 Stage 1 to the beginning of Version 4 Stage 2 Business System Options (BSO)*

At this point in both Versions 3 and 4 the current environment has been analysed. In Version 4 a logical view of the current services has also been produced. Before work can begin on Version 4 Stage 2, the Version 3 current system dataflow diagrams should be logicalised using the Version 4 logicalisation techniques.

Some further adaptation of Version 3 products is necessary but this should be minimal as the use of the logical data modelling and data flow modelling techniques in Stage 1 has changed very little between the two versions. The new requirements definition technique drives the analysis in Stage 1 of Version 4 so it will be necessary to ensure that the Version 3 Stage 1 products are focussed on eliciting requirements. The additional work required is described in more detail in Annex A.

Chapter 6
Migration of SSADM projects

Advantages of migrating at this point are:

- the amount of rework necessary is not significant
- most of the Version 4 benefits can still be realised by migrating at this early point in the method

Cut-over point 3 *From the end of Version 3 BSOs to the beginning of Version 4 Requirements Specification Module (RS)*

A Business System Option has been selected at this point in both Versions. The next step in Version 4 is to amend the products of the Requirements Analysis Module to reflect the Selected BSO and add more detail to the definition of requirements contained in the Analysis of Requirements.

In Stage 2 of SSADM Version 3 the logical system is defined, the BSO to be taken forward is selected, and the required system is specified in detail. The equivalent point to the beginning of the Requirements Specification Module falls in the middle of Stage 2 in Version 3. Even though BSOs fall in the middle of a Version 3 stage it is still a major decision point in the method as options are presented to the Project Board for selection. Consideration should be given to migrating from Version 3 at this point.

Some rework will be necessary, but none of major significance. The BSO documentation in both versions is comparable and other differences are mainly notational. See Annex A for a fuller description of the additional work necessary.

Advantages of migrating at this point are:

- many of the benefits of Version 4 can be gained by migrating at this point. The Requirements Specification Module of Version 3 is where many of the new Version 4 techniques and other improvements are introduced (function definition, specification prototyping, entity-event modelling, some of dialogue design is carried out, relational data analysis takes place in Stage 3, Enquiry Access Paths are produced)
- it is in this module that the user requirements are drawn out and captured in the Requirements Specification.

Cut-over point 4 — *From the end of Version 3 Stage 2 to the beginning of the Logical System Specification Module (LS)*

At this point both versions of the method have specified the user requirements but there are several important differences between the two versions of the method at this point:

- RDA is carried out before this point in Version 4 (in Step 340)
- new techniques for logical database process design and dialogue design are used in the Logical System Specification Module.

There is some quite significant reworking of documentation required at this point to fully convert to Version 4. This is described fully in Annex A, but to summarise:

- the Version 3 functions need to be validated to ensure they conform to and are documented to the level required by Version 4
- I/O Structures must be produced for the functions
- RDA must be carried out and this may result in some rework of the ELHs
- operations must be added to the ELHs
- Effect Correspondence Diagrams must be produced
- Enquiry Access Paths (EAPs) must be produced
- if dialogues have already been documented using Version 3 standards they may need to be reworked.

Advantages of migrating at this point are:

- there are significant improvements in logical database process design, with the introduction of Enquiry Process Models and Update Process Models, and in logical dialogue design which can be exploited by migrating at this point

- full Version 4 training can be staggered with staff being given workshop-type training on the new techniques, thus reducing the initial training cost
- staff can be given training when they need it.

Cut-over point 5 — *From the end of Version 3 Stage 3 to the beginning of Version 4 Stage 5 Logical Design*

This option is very similar to the previous option, except that at this point in Version 3 Technical Options (TOs) have been carried out. In Version 4 Technical System Options (TSOs) do not take place until Stage 4 in the LS Module. Therefore only Stage 5 of the Version 4 LS Module needs to be performed if migration takes place at this point.

If migration takes place at this point the Version 4 benefit of being able to perform logical design and TSOs in parallel is lost. As in the previous option there will be a significant amount of rework required to be in a position to move forward with Version 4, see above.

Advantages of migrating at this point are:

- there are significant improvements in logical database process design, with the introduction of Enquiry Process Models and Update Process Models, and in logical dialogue design which can be taken advantage of by migrating at this point
- full Version 4 training can be staggered with staff being given workshop-type training on these new techniques, thus reducing the initial training cost
- staff can be given training when they need it

The additional work required is described in more detail in Annex A.

Cut-over point 6 — *From the end of Version 3 Stages 4 and 5 to the beginning of Version 4 Physical Design Module (PD)*

It may not seem worthwhile to migrate to Version 4 at this late stage in the project. However, Stage 6 of Version 4 describes an approach rather than a prescriptive set of rules to be followed. Step 610, Prepare for Physical Design, enables the designers to study the implementation environment and to make decisions about how the facilities available in that environment can best be exploited. Once these decisions have been made the Stage 6 activities are planned in detail and the products to be delivered defined. This approach could be used with Version 3 documentation as the input.

This volume cannot provide the detail of how the Version 3 products are transformed in physical design.

Advantages of migrating at this point are:

- the approach to physical design has been improved with the recognition that Stage 6 must be tailored to reflect the target environment
- Stage 6 is designed to be tailored so this approach can be extended to accommodate the input of Version 3 products rather than Version 4 products.

7 Checklist

The move from Version 3 to 4 should be well-considered, well-managed and controlled. Each SSADM project is different, as is each project environment. Exactly how and when the move from Version 3 to Version 4 is effected depends on the type of project, its stage of development and the project environment. Each organisation must consider, for each project, the benefits to be gained against the costs to the project in terms of time and then choose the best migration route.

These are the major points to consider when planning migration:

- is there management commitment to Version 4?
- has the interface between the project management method and Version 4 been defined?
- in the particular circumstances that prevail, what is the preferred approach to migration?
- is there the opportunity to use Version 4 from scratch on a pilot project? If not, at which point in the project's life would it be best to migrate?
- which projects would reap most benefit from migrating?
- what will the impact of converting to Version 4 be on project timescales?
- is the budget available and can training be organised for practitioners, managers and users?
- is the budget available for consultancy support?
- are staff of the right calibre available?
- is there CASE tool support available?
- have the necessary standards been set?

To realise fully the benefits of SSADM Version 4 can only be realised if the move from Version 3 to 4 must be well planned.

Annexes

A Redocumentation needed for each cut-over point

A1 Cut-over point 1

From the end of the Version 3 Feasibility Study to the beginning of the Version 4 Requirements Analysis Module

Migrating from Version 3 to Version 4 of SSADM at the end of a Version 3 Feasibility Study is relatively straightforward. This equates to the project starting in Version 4 at the beginning of Requirements Analysis Module (RA). At this point in both versions of the method a Feasibility Study will usually have taken place. The aim of the study is to determine whether the proposed information system can meet the business needs and whether the investment needed to produce the system is justified.

In Version 4 of SSADM the inputs to Stage 1 are:

- Feasibility Report
- Project Initiation Document
- Reports from previous studies.

Of these three only the Feasibility Report is an SSADM product. The Feasibility Report in Version 4 is defined in more detail than the equivalent Feasibility Study Report produced by Version 3. The two reports should contain similar information, even if they are structured or documented differently.

The Annexes to the Version 4 Feasibility Report contain some supporting SSADM system documentation for the selected option, comprising:

- current and required DFDs (developed to at the most two levels)
- an Overview Logical Data Structure
- an initial User Catalogue defining the users of the system
- an initial Requirements Catalogue documenting new requirements.

Migrating from SSADM Version 3 to Version 4

The SSADM system documentation products included in the Version 3 Feasibility Report are:

- a Problems/Requirements List and a Base Constraints List
- Required DFDs down to level 2 with Elementary Function Descriptions
- a required Logical Data Structure with Entity Descriptions
- an outline Technical Environment Description for the proposed system
- an initial Event Catalogue.

In addition both reports contain some sort of Cost/Benefit Analysis, an Impact Analysis and a Project Plan, plus other management information.

Additional work required to move from Version 3 to 4

Step 110, Establish Analysis Framework, requires the practitioner to assimilate information from previous studies and to prepare for more detailed analysis. This step assumes a preliminary study has been carried out, but not necessarily an SSADM Feasibility Study. The inputs to the step are reviewed to ensure that the conclusions of previous studies are still relevant. There are tasks in this step to create a Context Diagram, Current Physical Data Flow Diagram and Overview Logical Data Structure and to document system requirements in the Requirements Catalogue. The Version 3 SSADM Feasibility Study produces a Problems/Requirements List and a Base Constraints List, which can be reviewed and form the basis of the Requirements Catalogue produced in Stage 1 of Version 4. The Context diagram, Current Physical DFD and Overview LDS can be developed from the DFDs and the Logical Data Structure in the Version 3 Feasibility Study Report.

Some additional work may be necessary if a Version 3 Feasibility Study is carried out rather than a Version 4 study, but there will be less work than if no Feasibility Study is done at all.

Annex A
Redocumentation needed for each cut-over point

A2   Cut-over point 2   **From the end of Version 3 Stage 1 to the beginning of Version 4 Stage 2 Business System Options**

An analysis of the current environment is carried out in both Versions 3 and 4 of the method, but in Version 4 a logical view of the current services is also produced. Before work can begin on the Version 4 Stage 2 the Version 3 current system DFDs should be logicalised using the Version 4 logicalisation techniques. Another difference between the two stages is that in Version 4 the analysis of the current is directed at eliciting requirements through the requirements definition technique.

In Version 4 of SSADM the inputs required by Stage 2 are:

- the Current Services Description comprising,
    - Current Environment Logical Data Model
    - Context Diagram
    - Logical Data Flow Model
    - Logical Data Store/Entity cross-reference
- Project Initiation Document
- Requirements Catalogue
- User Catalogue.

The SSADM products output from Version 3 Stage 1 are:

- DFDs of the current physical system
- Elementary Function Descriptions
- Entity Descriptions
- Logical Data Structure
- Problems/Requirements List.

Additional work required to move from Version 3 to 4

The rework necessary is listed by technique and where it is significant the techniques are placed in the order in which the rework should be undertaken. Within the descriptions of each technique, where appropriate, an indication is given of the interdependencies in the rework. The redocumentation required for each project must be planned in detail.

49

Migrating from SSADM Version 3 to Version 4

Data Flow Modelling	The Version 3 DFDs must be logicalised before BSOs are carried out. This is not additional work as it would have been done as the next activity in Version 3. The DFDs should be logicalised using the Version 4 guidance and at the same time should be brought up to the Version 3 documentation standards. A Logical Data Store/Entity cross-reference is produced as part of the logicalisation.
	The Data Flow Model in Version 4 consists of the Data Flow Diagrams, plus the supporting documentation of Elementary Process Descriptions (EPDs), External Entity Descriptions and I/O Descriptions. In Version 3 at this point only the DFDs and the Elementary Function Descriptions (equivalent to the EPDs) exist. There are minor notational changes in Version 4 DFDs which will have to be incorporated in the logical DFDs. A CASE tool could make these amendments automatically.
	There will be some more significant additional work as I/O Descriptions and External Entity Descriptions will have to be created from scratch at logicalisation. The Elementary Function Descriptions must be checked to ensure that they are to the same standard as Version 4 Elementary Process Descriptions.
	If DFDs are produced to illustrate the Business System Options these should be produced to the standard described in the Version 4 manual.
Dialogue Design	One of the inputs to Version 4 BSOs is the User Catalogue, which lists the on-line users and their tasks. This must be created before Version 4 BSOs are begun from the Version 3 documentation (DFDs and LDS, PRL) and through discussion with users.
Logical Data Modelling	Updating the Version 3 data model to Version 4 standard can be delayed until Stage 3 of Version 4 when the Required System LDM is produced. If data models are produced to illustrate the Business System Options these should be done to Version 4 standard.
	The Current Environment LDM in Version 4 comprises the LDS, Entity Descriptions and Relationship Descriptions. The LDS notation in Version 4 is different from that in Version 3. Some of the differences are

intended to aid identification – for example, entity boxes in Version 4 are round-cornered. Some of the changes may mean some further analysis is required. For example, the notation for relationships in Version 4 allows the practitioner to be more precise about the type of relationship between two entities. The Version 3 Logical Data Structure for the current environment will not have all the information required to carry out a straight conversion to Version 4 notation.

Relationship Descriptions do not exist in Version 3, so these will have to be created from scratch for the Required System LDM in Stage 3.The Entity Descriptions from the Version 3 Logical Data Structure will have to be updated with relationship information for the Version 4 Required System LDM.

Requirements Definition   The Requirements Catalogue entries in Version 4 enable the practitioner to document service level requirements in the form of non-functional requirements against a functional requirement. In Version 3 this information is not documented in the Version 3 Problems/Requirements List (PRL) until Step 210. This additional work can be postponed until Stage 3 when the requirements are specified fully.

A3   Cut-over point 3

From the end of Version 3 BSOs to the beginning of the Version 4 Requirements Specification Module (RS)

At this point in both Versions a Business System Option has been selected. The next step in Version 4 is to amend the products of the Requirements Analysis Module to reflect the Selected BSO and add more detail to the definition of requirements contained in the Analysis of Requirements.

In Stage 2 of SSADM Version 3 the logical system is defined, the BSO to be taken forward is selected, and the required system is specified in detail. The equivalent point to the beginning of the Requirements Specification Module falls in the middle of Stage 2 in Version 3. Even though BSOs fall in the middle of a Version 3 stage it is still a major decision point in the method as options are presented to the Project Board for selection. Consideration should be given to migrating at this point.

Migrating from SSADM Version 3 to Version 4

The Requirements Specification Module requires the following Version 4 products:

- Selected BSO
- Logical DFM
- Current Environment LDM
- Requirements Catalogue
- Logical Data Store/Entity Cross Reference
- User Catalogue.

In Version 3 of SSADM at the end of Step 220, Identify and Select from BSOs, the following products are produced:

- Selected BSO
- Logical DFDs with Elementary Function Descriptions
- Logical Data Structure and Entity Descriptions
- Retrievals Catalogue
- Problems/Requirements List
- Base Constraints List
- Data Store/Entity Cross-Reference.

Additional work required to move from Version 3 to 4	The rework necessary is listed by technique and where it is significant the techniques are placed in the order in which the rework should be undertaken. Within the descriptions of each technique, where appropriate, an indication is given of the interdependencies in the rework. The redocumentation required for each project must be planned in detail.
Business System Options	The Selected BSO documentation in both versions of the method is comparable.
Data Flow Modelling	The Data Flow Model in Version 4 consists of the Data Flow Diagrams, plus the supporting documentation of Elementary Process Descriptions (EPDs), External Entity Descriptions and I/O Descriptions. Only the DFDs and the Elementary Function Descriptions (equivalent to the EPDs) exist at this point in Version 3. There are minor

Annex A
Redocumentation needed for each cut-over point

notational changes in Version 4 DFDs which will have to be incorporated in the Required System DFDs. There will be some more significant additional work in Step 310, Define Required System Processing, as I/O Descriptions and External Entity Descriptions will have to be created from scratch for the required system.

The Version 4 Logical Data Store/Entity Cross Reference and the Version 3 Data Store/Entity Cross-Reference are equivalent documents, so there will be no reworking necessary.

Dialogue Design   There is no equivalent document to the User Catalogue in Version 3. In Step 310 where User Roles are identified from the User Catalogue it will be necessary to identify users of the system and their tasks and from that information derive the User Roles. It is not necessary at this point to formally document this information in a User Catalogue.

Logical Data Modelling   The Current Environment LDM in Version 4 comprises the LDS, Entity Descriptions and Relationship Descriptions. The LDS notation in Version 4 is different from that in Version 3. Some of the differences are intended to aid identification – for example entity boxes in Version 4 are round-cornered. Some of the changes may mean some further analysis is required. For example, the notation for relationships in Version 4 allows the practitioner to be more precise about the type of relationship between two entities. The Version 3 Logical Data Structure for the current environment will not have all the information required to carry out a straight conversion to Version 4 notation. Relationship Descriptions do not exist in Version 3 so these will have to be created from scratch for the Required System LDM. The Entity Descriptions from the Version 3 Logical Data Structure will have to be updated with relationship information for the Version 4 Required System LDM.

Requirements Definition   The Requirements Catalogue entries in Version 4 enable the practitioner to document service level requirements in the form of non-functional requirements against a functional requirement. In Version 3 this information is documented in Step 210, but it will be recorded informally in the description of the requirement in the Problems/Requirements List.

A4	Cut-over point 4	**From the end of Version 3 Stage 2 to the beginning of the Logical System Specification Module (LS)**

At this point both versions of the method have specified the user requirements but there are several important differences between the two versions of the method at this point:

- RDA is carried out before this point in Version 4 (in Step 340)
- new techniques for logical database process design and dialogue design are used in the Logical System Specification Module of Version 4
- operations are added to ELHs in Version 4 but not in Version 3.

Additional work required to move from Version 3 to Version 4	The rework necessary is listed by technique and where it is significant the techniques are placed in the order in which the rework should be undertaken. Within the descriptions of each technique, where appropriate, an indication is given of the interdependencies in the rework. The redocumentation required for each project must be planned in detail.
Function Definition	At the end of Stage 2 in Version 3 functions will have been recorded in the Function Catalogues, both on-line and off-line. These functions should be reviewed to ensure they are documented to the level expected in Version 4. I/O Structures should be created for the functions as they are required for both RDA and dialogue design.
Relational Data Analysis	In Version 4 Relational Data Analysis is carried out in Stage 3, whereas in Version 3 it does not take place until Stage 4. Before Stage 5 of Version 4 can begin RDA has to be carried out and the results used to update the logical data model. The ELHs need to be reviewed to take account of the amendments made to the LDM as a result of RDA. I/O Structures are created in Function Definition in Stage 3 and these are the main input to RDA. RDA can be carried out as in Version 3 without these I/O Structures, but as they are also the basis from which Dialogue Structures are produced in Step 510 it is worth creating the I/O Structures.

Annex A
Redocumentation needed for each cut-over point

Technical System Options	In Version 3 Technical Options (TOs) are carried out in Stage 3, in Version 4 Technical System Options (TSOs) take place in Stage 4. The technique is not significantly different in the two versions of the method, so Version 4 TSOs can be produced using the Version 3 products as input.
Dialogue Design	User dialogues are defined in Step 510. In Version 4 the dialogues to be developed are identified in Step 330 and documented in the User Role/Function Matrix. In Version 3 dialogues were developed for each on-line event and enquiry. In Version 4 dialogues are created at the function level. If logical dialogues have already been created according to Version 3 standards, a decision has to be made whether or not to convert these dialogues to Version 4 notation. The Version 3 dialogues can be taken forward to physical design. If the dialogues have not already been documented then they should be documented to Version 4 standards.
Preparation for Logical Database Process Design	Update Process Models are produced in Step 520, Define Update Processes. In order to do this Effect Correspondence Diagrams must be produced from the ELHs. The Version 3 ELHs must be reviewed to ensure they have been developed with the same amount of rigour as is expected in Version 4. Operations must be added to the ELHs to complete them to Version 4 standard. In Version 4 the ELH analysis technique has been upgraded to feed into the new techniques of effect correspondence diagramming and logical database process design.
	In Step 530 Enquiry Process Models are created. In Version 4 these are developed from Enquiry Access Paths produced in Stage 3. An Enquiry Access Path must be created for each retrieval documented in the Version 3 Retrieval Catalogue.

A5 Cut-over point 5

From the end of Version 3 Stage 3 to the beginning of Version 4 Stage 5 Logical Design

In Version 3 Technical Options (TOs) are carried out before logical design. In Version 4 they are carried out in parallel with the logical design activity. This option is similar to the previous option as far as the reworking of the Required System Specification products is concerned.

Additional work required to move from Version 3 to Version 4	The rework necessary is listed by technique and where it is significant the techniques are placed in the order in which the rework should be undertaken. Within the descriptions of each technique, where appropriate, an indication is given of the interdependencies in the rework. The redocumentation required for each project must be planned in detail.
Function Definition	At the end of Stage 2 in Version 3 functions will have been recorded in the Function Catalogues, both on-line and off-line. These functions should be reviewed to ensure they are documented to the level expected in Version 4. I/O Structures should be created for the functions as they are required for both RDA and dialogue design.
Technical System Options	In Version 3 Technical System Options (TOs) are carried out in Stage 3, in Version 4 Technical System Options (TSOs) take place in Stage 4. The technique is not significantly different in the two versions of the method. The Version 3 TO documentation should be comprehensive enough to be input to Version 4 physical design. The first step in Stage 6 is to plan the physical design activity, so there is an opportunity to assess the Version 3 TO documentation at that point.
	The following additional work is done to bring the Required System Specification to the level required so that Version 4 logical design can take place in Stage 5. It is the same as the additional work required for option 4.
Relational Data Analysis	In Version 4 Relational Data Analysis is carried out in Stage 3, whereas in Version 3 it does not take place until Stage 4. RDA has to be carried out and the results used to update the logical data model before Version 4 Stage 5, Logical Design, can begin. The ELHs need to be reviewed to take account of the amendments made to the LDM as a result of RDA. I/O Structures are created in Function Definition in Stage 3 and these are the main input to RDA. RDA can be carried out as in Version 3 without these I/O Structures, but as they are also the basis from which Dialogue Structures are produced in Step 510 it is worth creating the I/O Structures.

	Dialogue Design	In Step 510 user dialogues are defined. In Version 4 the dialogues to be developed are identified in Step 330 and documented in the User Role/Function Matrix. In Version 3 dialogues were developed for each on-line event and enquiry. In Version 4 dialogues are created at the function level. If logical dialogues have already been created according to Version 3 standards a decision has to be made whether or not to convert these dialogues to Version 4 notation. The Version 3 dialogues can be taken forward to physical design. If the dialogues have not already been documented then they should be documented to Version 4 standards.
	Preparation for Logical Database Process Design	In Step 520, Define Update Processes, Update Process Models are produced. In order to do this Effect Correspondence Diagrams must be produced from the ELHs. The Version 3 ELHs must be reviewed to ensure they have been developed with the same amount of rigour as is expected in Version 4. Operations must be added to the ELHs to complete them to Version 4 standard. In Version 4 the ELH analysis technique has been upgraded to feed into the new techniques of effect correspondence diagramming and logical database process design.
		In Step 530 Enquiry Process Models are created. In Version 4 these are developed from Enquiry Access Paths produced in Stage 3. An Enquiry Access Path must be created for each retrieval documented in the Version 3 Retrieval Catalogue.
A6	Cut-over point 6	**From the end of Version 3 Stages 4 and 5 to the beginning of Version 4 Physical Design Module (PD)**
		No detailed advice can be given as the rework necessary to migrate at this point in a project's life is dependent on the implementation environment. Because of the large amount of rework and the differing philosophies of Version 3 and Version 4, it is not likely that migration would be undertaken at this point.

Bibliography

SSADM documentation The SSADM Version 4 Reference Manual is published by NCC and is available from The Publications Manager, National Computer Centre Ltd, Oxford Road, Manchester M1 7ED. ISBN: 1 85554 004 5.

Information Systems Guides The Information Systems Guides, published by CCTA, are available from John Wiley & Sons Ltd, Baffins Lane, Chichester PO19 1UD.

The following guide is referenced in this publication:

> A2: Strategic Planning for Information Systems
> ISBN: 0 471 92522 5

Information Systems Engineering Library The Information Systems Engineering Library volumes, published by CCTA, are available from HMSO Publications Centre, PO Box 276, London SW8 5DT.

IS Planning Subject Guides The IS Planning Subject Guides are available from Library, CCTA, Riverwalk House, 157–161 Millbank, London SW1 4RT.

The following subject guide is referenced in this publication:

> Prioritisation
> ISBN: 0 946683 44

Glossary

Activity Description — Activities within SSADM Steps all effect transformations in one or more products. The description of an 'activity' details what the transformation is, the inputs, the references and the participants.

CASE tool — Computer Aided Software Engineering tool. This is a tool which supports the application of development techniques during the SSADM modules, such as Logical Data Modelling or Data Flow Diagramming. Most CASE tools also provide an integrated repository which holds the information recorded on the objects (for example, entities) and in addition will normally provide facilities for reporting on the information and providing integrity checks.

CRAMM — CCTA Risk Analysis and Management Methodology - a methodology for assessing and managing risks in IT systems.

Dialogue Design — This is a technique. It is used to define the on-line activity of the system. Dialogues are identified as part of the Requirements Specification and then logically designed explicitly as part of the Logical Design. Physical dialogue design activities are undertaken during the physical design activities to complete the design prior to system implementation.

ECD — see *Effect Correspondence Diagramming*

Effect Correspondence Diagramming — This is a product that shows all the effects an event has on data within the system and how those effects impact upon each other. Effect Correspondence Diagrams provide the access path details for update function which is used in logical design activities.

Euromethod — A project to define a common approach to information systems development. The project grew out of discussions between CCTA and equivalent bodies in other EEC countries about the opportunities and benefits, for governments in the EEC, of common approaches.

Feasibility Study Module	This is a Structural Model element. The objective of this Module is to produce the Feasibility Report which will suggest the way ahead for the project. The activities form a short assessment of a proposed information system to determine whether the system would be feasible and appropriate to the business needs of the organisation. Feasibility is assessed in term of the managerial, business, financial, technological and cultural needs of the organisation. This Module has one Stage: Stage 0 - Feasibility.
FS	see *Feasibility Study Module*
Function Definition	This is a technique which identifies and documents functions which are the units of processing carried forward to physical design.
I/O Structure	This documents the input to and outputs from a function, or part of a function. It is document on I/O Structure Diagrams and I/O Structure Description.
LS	see *Logical System Specification Module*
Logical System Specification Module	This is a Structural Model Element. The objective of this Module is to produce the Logical System Specification. The Selected Technical System Option and the Technical Environment Description define the scope of the physical implementation. This details must be consistent with the Logical Design. This Module has two Stages: Stage 4 - Technical System Options and Stage 5 - Logical Design.
Module	This is a Structural Model Element. The SSADM framework requires a project to be sub-divided into a number of Modules each of which consists of one or more Stages. Each Module forms a distinct unit for management purposes. A Module has a defined set of products and activities, a finite lifespan and an organisational structure. The production of the defined end products, to agreed quality standards, signals the completion of the Module.
PD	see *Physical Design Module*
Physical Design Module	The objective of this Module is to produce the Physical Design for the system based on the Logical System Specification and the Physical Environment Specification – that is, it will be implementation dependent. This Module has one Stage: Stage 6 - Physical Design.

Glossary

PRINCE	PRojects IN Controlled Environments is a government developed methodology for project management with particular application to the management of Information Systems projects. It is a development of the PROMPT methodology which has been in use in government departments since 1983.
Product Breakdown Structures	Identifies the products which are required and which must be produced by a project. The document describes the system in a hierarchic way, decomposing it through a number of levels down to the components of each project.
PBS	see *Product Breakdown Structures*
Product Description	Describes the purpose, form and components of a product, and lists the quality criteria which apply to it.
RA	see *Requirements Analysis Module*
RDA	see *Relational Data Analysis*
Relational Data Analysis	This is a technique for deriving data structures which have the least redundant data and the most flexibility. The flexibility is achieved by breaking down the data groups into smaller groups without losing any of the original information. It is the objective of this technique to transform all relations into at least third normal form (3NF).
Requirements Analysis Module	This is a Structural Model Element. The objective of this module is to produce the Analysis of Requirements. Within this the Selected Business System Option will define the scope for further investigation. This Module has two Stages: Stage 1 - Investigation of Current Environment, and Stage 2 - Business System options.
Requirements Specification Module	This is a Structural Model element. The object of this module is to product the Requirements Specification. This module has one Stage: Stage 3 - Definition of Requirements.
RS	see *Requirements Specification Module*
SDM	Structured Design Method. A method to assist in the design of COBOL programmes.

Specification Prototyping	This is a technique used to identify and trap errors in the specification of the user requirement and to enhance them prior to detailed logical design activities being undertaken.
SSADM	The Structured Systems Analysis and Design Method is a non proprietary and publicly available method which provides a structured set of procedural, technical and documentation standards designed specifically for analysing business needs and undertaking software development.
Structural Model	This provides for SSADM a record of system processes and messages and material flows in the form of a flowchart drawn to highlight the sequencing, nesting and control of the processes and the converging and diverging of message and material flows.
Technical System Options	These are developed so that the system development direction can be chosen. Each option documents the function to be incorporated and details implementation requirements. Each description is textual with some planning information. Function elements are taken directly from the Requirements Specification.
TSO	see *Technical System Options*
User Catalogue	This provides a description of the on-line users of the proposed system. It includes details of job titles and the tasks undertaken by each of the identified users.
User Roles	A user role is defined as a collection of job holders who share a large proportion of common tasks. These tasks are recorded in the User Role document.

Printed in the United Kingdom for HMSO.
Dd295385 5/92 C8 G3390 10170